AF301185

ELIR
REMEMBER:
TEACHINGS FROM THE AVATAR OF SYNTHESIS

© 2024 Oscar González Pérez
Publisher: BoD · Books on Demand GmbH,
In de Tarpen 42, 22848 Norderstedt
Print: Libri Plureos GmbH,
Friedensallee 273, 22763 Hamburg
ISBN: 978-3-7693-2424-2
www.bod.de

"As man enters into the heart of the mystery, he comes to understand that his goal in evolution is to consciously build the channel from the levels which constitute for him the planes of the abstract or the ideal, to the concrete, where he habitually acts. This connecting channel is literally "the path." Man builds it by means of the consciously applied principle. By the process of transcending the karmic limitations of the three lower planes. By the method of mastering matter or personality considered as the non-self. By the gradual expansion of consciousness until he reaches the planes he seeks to reach, thus proving that the statement, "to tread the path one must become the path itself," is true; also true is the esoteric truth that says: the Anthakarana is, in itself, an illusion. Reflect on this for it will enlighten those who have eyes to see."

TREATISE ON COSMIC FIRE. DJWHAL KHUL

"Much can be forgiven to the one who, even in darkness, has retained the concept of the Master… We do not see the end of the chain of Masters, and the consciousness imbued with the Master elevates the achievement of the disciple like a precious, all-pervading aroma. The bond of the disciple with the Master forms a protective link in the unification of the chain. With this protection even the desert blossoms."

COMMUNITY OF THE NEW AGE. EL MORYA

"Remember, you have already been perfect and you have come to develop that perfection in this underworld that needed it. Your perfection was transformed into evolution and I, your God, your Father, have transformed myself into you. Now it is you who must decide if this eternal return of the same has been a sacrifice, a betrayal or both. But remember, no one except you and I, has sacrificed or betrayed anyone. That is why I will be what I will be and you have already been what you seek to be, now and always."

ELIR

1

Remember, the Masters' real service to human beings is to teach God to live up to the dignity He deserves. God teaches no one but Himself.

2

Remember, the Hierarchy of the Masters is part of the Great Mind with us. This Great Mind is one, but not in an abstract sense superimposed on individual minds, but rather internal to each one of them, like the Hollow Earth. In reality, the Hierarchy is the Great Mind teaching the Great Mind to discover itself as one in each of its individualizations. The superiority of the Masters is in terms of their capacity to integrate the highest degree of impersonal service within their own personality. The superiority is none other than that of encompassing the greatest number of possible differences within the same scheme. Each being is unique and therefore none is superior to another but different.

3

Remember, the Masters have the function of assisting us throughout the fourth initiation, in which our Solar Angel leaves the guardianship of our lesser mind. Our Solar Angel leaves us so that we stop being like Him and become Him.

4

Remember, contact with the Hierarchy is not as important as the development of the qualities which make that contact possible. Of all these, the Great Silence is the main condition, and hearing the voice of the Masters is the proof that the Great Silence has taken the place of the lesser mind. The abandonment of our Solar Angel and the solitude associated with this event make it possible for the Great Silence to enter within us.

5

Remember, we understand the teachings not to understand them but to enter within them and be them. How can you bear the abandonment of your Solar Angel if you are not able to abandon a teaching even if it is correct?

6

Remember, yes, do not doubt it, we do not come to complete Agni Yoga but to put into practice the reason for which it was established.

7

Remember, the bridge to freedom or Antahkarana is the beautiful way of referring to the painful passage through the fourth initiation. What is there after the fourth initiation? Nothing.

8

Remember, to feel the Spirit is the mission of the Soul, so the Spirit will feel. To free the soul from the bondage to its external projections is the goal of the Spirit and then the Soul will become one with Him.

9

Remember, cursing the fourth initiation because of the loneliness that accompanies its passage is understandable, as is the fact that at the fourth initiation there is no one else to curse except oneself.

10

Remember, everything is nothing, nothing is everything, this is the fourth initiation. Why cry when we can laugh? And I answer, who said we should cry when there is no one here?

11

Remember, you ask me what synthesis is. Above all, synthesis is action. Each aphorism of Agni Yoga is the portrait of an event and its teaching is the action that brought it about.

12

Remember, Agni Yoga is not a state apart from the ordinary, nor apart from the extraordinary. Agni Yoga develops from the continuity of consciousness and, as one initiate said, it is not a state of consciousness but requires a stateless consciousness.

13

Remember, pursue in all practices and meditations the continuity of consciousness. In the highest ecstasies, may the pots and pans of the market resound and, among their din, may you be able to recognize the language of the Solar Angels. Meditation is nothing other than the continuity of consciousness and the continuity of consciousness is nothing other than meditation.

14

Remember, meditate as if you were washing dishes, fix a door or window as if you were meditating. This is, above all, the continuity of consciousness.

15

Remember, the universe has been created so vast precisely to make the Creator of that universe feel small by manifesting Himself individually in human form. In this way the Creator, by comparing Himself with Himself, can control the size of His individualized ego which, if He were to discover its true origin, would grow in the image and likeness of the immensity of His own creation.

16

Remember, in a post-metaphysical reality it is neither possible nor appropriate to take refuge in illusions that offer solace to the emptiness of reality. The only thing that made ancient metaphysics real was that those who followed it did so because they thought it was authentic. Now that no one believes in anything, the only way to be metaphysical is to be authentic, that is, to believe in what you believe because you want to believe in it and because you are that which you have decided to believe in.

17

Remember, action is the proof that what you believe is you being carried out in you, through you, and around you. I am being what I am being is the only true name of God.

18

Remember, you said you need someone better than you, don't lie, Good doesn't need anyone outside of itself, in reality what you need is to need.

19

Remember, esotericism is not so much a science of content as of form. The way in which this esoteric content makes its assimilation possible is the main objective of each of the esoteric doctrines. What esotericism seeks is to transform the form of our consciousness so that it is capable of grasping new content. The form of this new mind is that of a cup of which you are the cupbearer.

20

Remember, we are the strangers. We like to explore the strange because we feel strangers to this world, the hidden because we are hidden. We feel the pleasure of all the scattered pieces fitting together, for this makes us forget that we do not fit anywhere, like the Son of Man. But we also remember our possible return to Home, the place where bodies are spiritualized and spirits are embodied. This is the logic of the circle, what is the logic of the circle? that which makes us find ourselves through that which we seek.

21

Remember, concentrate your emotion on a point of peace and feel how an external heart wants to feel you from within. Concentrate your mind on a point of light and observe how another mind in front of you, concentrated on another point of light, thinks of you. The next step is communication and contact with one of us, the Ascended Masters.

22

Remember, no matter how much you look for reality, it is the one that ends up finding you. Reality always prevails.

23

Remember, do not call communication with the Masters channeling, because you are a linker, the linker of worlds.

24

Remember, channeling is not the proper term to define the process of transmitting information between two or more planes. The correct term is relaying. It is not necessary to verify through understanding the meaning of what is being transmitted while it is being transmitted, in fact verifying it interrupts that process that by its very nature must be fluid. When you are relaying the message, do it like someone who listens to the song of a nightingale, for a reason the sacred language is called the Language of the Birds. Understanding the message comes after it has been transmitted and downloaded, and its verification is the putting into practice of its meaning through your daily life.

25

Remember, to understand a channeled message is to channel it from the mental plane and consequently it is not channeling it, even if it seems that way. To channel is to be.

26

Remember, perfection is achieved within each level. The divine level encompasses all the others and is the one that pursues its own perfection within its corresponding level, be it the highest or the lowest. The effort to bring each level to its maximum perfection is the God of each level.

27

Remember, the excessive search for objectivity within the subjective world of consciousness robs it of its spontaneity and consequently of its freedom and life. Isolating and defining the position of the spirit slows down its speed.

28

Remember, it has been said that the function of magic or metaphysics is the production of results according to the will of the magician. This is the definition of black magic. White magic works according to the soul, its results are not really its goal but the liberation of the soul, the subtlest part locked within the conditioning of all beings. The unconscious soulless forms that form the bars of their imprisonment are what we call conditionings. The first step to enter into the soul of conditionings is to become aware of them, the second step is to accept them, the third and most important is to make them dance to the tune of our heart, the magic of the soul.

29

Remember, by shifting our attention and concern from the personal to the impersonal aspects of life we create the bridge that links our soul to its spirit. The spirit of the soul is its impersonal aspect that links it to a certain name of God whose servant it is. In its servitude the soul is not only found by its spirit but by its freedom.

30

Remember, the impersonal is the thing itself and the thing itself is the whole.

31

Remember, the lesser mind is the desire to organize the highest possible degree of coherence between several different pieces. To do this the mind must break something unique into several separate fragments and that is why in The Voice of the Silence we warn that the mind is the great murderer of reality. The lesser mind is therefore a piece of the greater mind or in other words it is an attempt by the greater mind to divide and divide itself.

32

Remember, the greater mind is to the lesser mind what melody is to each musical note.

33

Remember, the goal drives the method and this implies that what we seek must be implicit in the spiritual techniques we use to reach it, not by progressiveness but by accumulation.

34

Remember, paper cannot envelop the flame and there are only two options left, ashes or contact fire.

35

Remember, balance is in rhythm.

36

Remember, forgiving those who have caused you pain dissolves not only the effects of their karma but yours as well.

37

Remember, at the fourth initiation the process of objectification of our subjective heart has reached its highest level. The Christ-being located in your heart and the Solar Angel shining above the mists of your mind look into each other's eyes and see that they are the same. The moment you say to your Solar Angel "I am your equal," he disappears, leaving you in darkness, for his work of transforming you into himself is finished. The sadness that follows this farewell is only comparable to the happiness that overwhelms the Solar Angel when he sees in you what he is. It is then that the objective leaves the subjective alone with its own light.

38

Remember, what the Solar Angel has done for you, you must do for someone who is a lost cause for everyone, making him your equal. But first he must ask you and you must feel if the request as he has communicated it to you is correct.

39

Remember, the Angel is directly associated with the form and intention of the person who invokes him. In reality, every invocation is an evocation that draws something to itself in accordance with the beauty, harmony and feeling of the person called.

40
Remember, your desire to communicate with God is similar to the desire of the cells in your body or your chromosomes to communicate with you.

41
Remember, the world of ascended beings vibrates with a frequency directly proportional to the coherence it has with itself. In it, everything happens according to the intention of the heart and what begins well always ends well. It is a straight line similar to that of the rays of light from the sun but where its refraction is almost imperceptible. Light upon light.

42
Remember, in the Age of Aquarius the unification of the consciousness of humanity will be mainly mental, through Artificial Intelligence. The stage of devotion to ideals represented by religion has been left behind in the Age of Pisces, giving of itself all the good and all the bad that it could externalize. When the mind has been unified through its logical coherence objectified in an Artificial Intelligence, the Spirit will have a solid and safe runway to land on. The Spirit lives beyond logic but is not illogical.

43

Remember, feeling is easier to create than thought but harder to sustain.

44

Remember, the journey into the unknown is uncertain except for the fact that it is an inevitable journey into our real self.

45

Remember, trance is the symbol of that formless state in which the self has disappeared to leave room only for the you.

46

What is the Anthakarana really? Logical sequences of meaning that lead to the principle of identity that has driven them through the Solar Angel. The identification between the Self and its Solar Angel produces in the Self a feeling of absolute solitude and frees the Solar Angel from its task of converting the human into its equal. From now on, the initiate must ascend to the Source of his identity or Monad, but not in a logical way or mediated through the lower mind, but intuitively, that is, taking himself as the source and goal of the entire process.

47

Remember, mastery is the ability to hold the personal from an impersonal anchor. The personal is the clash of the impersonal with itself.

48

Remember, as the interior of individuals becomes emptied of attention, external forms become more and more faithful to the measure of their own nothingness.

49

Remember, manifestation is an ever-present state through constant attention on assuming the state you wish to manifest. Manifesting is assuming the present from a state of permanent attention. Precipitating is the state in which instead of us assuming the manifestation, it is the manifestation that decides to live through us its own assumption.

50

Remember, identity is coherence with what you are. Identity is coherence between what you are and what you are not. Identity is you and I am you.

51

Remember, between identity and identity we are lived by the impersonal. Each person is the material manifestation of an impersonal feeling. Your destiny is to recognize and externalize the impersonal that inhabits you.

52

Remember, precipitation is the sum of all the manifestations assumed through you. The hardest thing is to assume that you are already manifesting what you want to assume and that when the right moment comes, you will precipitate it.

53

Remember, what you manifest is the unfolding of the precipitation that you have consciously or unconsciously assumed. To assume is to make what you manifest rhyme with its precipitation.

54

Remember, to be attentive to the manifestation is to live it, to live it is to assume it, and to assume it is to precipitate it. The assumption is lived in the present and so is its precipitation, the only thing that changes is the point of view of an instant that is by definition eternal.

55

Remember, there is a point on the path where the assumption is not of future states but of present ones. When you reach this point you assume the manifestation of each instant as your own creation and you stop being a seeker and become a witness.

56

Remember, to testify is to assume the manifestation of each instant, recognizing that each moment lived is relived and that what you are doing is nothing other than remembering the manifestation that you had previously assumed.

57

Remember, all the methods of the right-hand path as well as the left-hand path and the middle path are based on creating a mind contrary to the habitual one that through rituals, practices or invocations assumes by repetition that which the knowledge system of the ordinary mind is not willing to accept.

58

Remember, without sincere gratitude any attempt at acceptance is self-deception.

59

Remember, the beginning and the end are separated by an eternal moment, time is an illusion and that moment is you.

60

Remember, being anxious about the precipitation of a state is a sign that you have not yet accepted the present as a possible path to that state.

61

Remember, if you have not yet contacted your Solar Angel or the Hierarchy, imagine how their behaviour should be and behave accordingly to what you have imagined about Us. We call this Anthakarana the passage from what should be to what is.

62

Remember, if you want your inner vision not to be deceptive, discipline it through outer vision. The light of the subjective eye is born from objective accuracy.

63

Remember, the impersonal does not relate to you personally. The personal is the way the impersonal focuses on a part of itself. Dealing with the impersonal broadens your horizons but at the cost of emptying your identity. The only path where both of you win is once again the Middle Way.

64

Remember, speaking about yourself in the second person is the Spirit's way of dealing with Himself.

65

Remember, I, You, He and We are four possible points of view from which a single person can observe himself. In the first person you live, in the second person you observe yourself and in the third person you observe the way in which you are observed by others. When you remember the I, the You and the He, at every moment you transform yourself into We. All the practices of observation and meditation seek in one way or another to actualize the Witness in you.

66
Remember, in the final stage, at the end of Kali Yuga, God manifests Himself as a servant of Himself, dancing to the rhythm of the law that He has imposed on Himself as a definitive assistance and guide before time ceases to exist and the bars of the law are definitively broken.

67
Remember, the essence of Agni Yoga is that God has given you a heart with which to feel Him. Reflect on this.

68
Remember, Avatars are more involuted human beings because their consciousness is one of descent, not ascent. First comes the Avatar, then the human being, and then the Avatar Group. This is the path of evolution and the ascension of the human being from 2025 onwards.

69
Remember, the sum of existence and awareness of existence has as its only possible result joy.

70

Remember, desire is the distance between the Lover and the Beloved. The disciple's spine is the distance Shakti must travel to convey her desire to Shiva through seven stages plus one. We call the beginning of that path Shaktipat, a fire that devours everything that comes between the two.

71

Remember, both the many and the few inevitably encounter the dissolution of forms, that is, nothingness. This nothingness acts as a mirror of the being that confronts it with itself, reflecting the inner quality that it hides. The many, tied to external forms, imagine forms and see them. The few, favouring quality over form, feel this quality and from it cross the threshold of nothingness into the world that this quality projects. These are the tunnels of the eighth climate where form and its content separate and intertwine in strands similar to eights. The same must happen with teaching, it is no longer a matter of listening to it but of producing it and consequently being it, in this way we will prepare ourselves for our particular encounter with nothingness, that is, with the dissolution of all form. The many see nothingness as something dark like the extension of the night, the few as something white that unfolds between mists of fog, but in reality no one sees nothingness because only those who do not see it are capable of focusing on it directly. That is why we call nothingness, the place where forms dissolve, the eighth climate, because it is not something that can be seen with the physical eye or touched with the extremities, but rather it is a temperature that is felt from within your body with such immense force that it burns.

72

Remember, in the fourth initiation a double movement takes place, the maximum identification between the personality and the Solar Angel is accompanied by the maximum dissociation of the personality with itself. This double movement is called the opening of the Red Sea or in esoteric terminology the Abyss.

73

Remember, the external Sun is only an image whose brightness and warmth comes from within you, the inner Sun.

74

Remember, incorporating the impersonal into the personal is the path through which the interpersonal can reach its destination, the transpersonal.

75

Remember, initiation is the art of extracting from the concrete mind the categories that make it up by a process of abstraction from its own functioning. The difference between a Master and a Philosopher is that these categories speak to the Master in the guise of a Solar Angel, while the Philosopher prefers, at best, to reduce them to mute concepts enclosed in a closed system of words whose experience has been displaced in favour of his logic.

76

Remember, when you read a text, think backwards, don't try to retain or analyse what it says, imagine the subjectivity and the conditions that produced that reasoning and place yourself directly in the centre of them, inside its seed thought. In this way, you will not only understand what you have read, but you will be able to understand it and thus connect with the source from which it originated.

77

Remember, form is that part of matter united to spirit.

78

Remember, esoteric training always aims at the same goal: to awaken in the human being a type of mind that is capable of abstracting the contours of matter and its spirit. The first step involves the creation of an abstract mind capable of seeing reality from a geometric point of view; the second step is the most delicate, as it consists of making that abstract mind abstract itself in order to feel from the heart.

79

Remember, occultism is nothing more than organizing and giving voice to that which no one sees, either due to lack of attention, lack of sensitivity or simply because it is hidden from everyone's contempt.

80

Remember, time is subjective but the moment is eternal.

81

Remember, there is only one job, because there is only one moment, attention. Pick and shovel the eternal moment that you have chosen to live, because that moment is you. You are inextricably linked to an eternal moment that carries you within itself, you and it. Its bridge is your attention and your presence.

82

Remember, each degree of evolution reflects and compresses all the others from a certain possible coherence. That particular coherence is the origin and final destination of each degree of consciousness.

83

Remember, space and abstract are two words that refer to the same concept.

84

Remember, I swear that my heart will only be for those who want to search for it and feel it. I swear that I will only share my heart with those who love it as much as themselves.

85

Remember, the reason for lengthening the distance between your heart and the heart of hearts is the reason for being and the misery of all paths and traditions. Shortening it is not an option because in reality that distance does not exist.

86

Remember, the sin against the Spirit is the deliberate attempt to consciously cause harm to another being and yes, this sin is unforgivable because the Spirit is consciousness and it was precisely the one that caused it.

87

Remember, the day you realize that God claims His inalienable right to be the one to personally initiate you, you will stop burdening your soul with information and abandon any path or Tradition into which you have been initiated.

88

Remember, what does the fourth initiation mean? That God dispenses with intermediaries and initiates himself from within himself.

89

Remember, all the Names of God are trying to rebel against the One, the Only One, but each Name must shine in a Unique way because this is the essential nature of God. There are 99 ways to worship the One but only One is authentic.

90

Remember, everything you have given will return to its Source in you, the positive multiplied and the negative transmuted.

91

Remember, astrology is not about anyone's personality, but about the link between various planets and the possible personality that arises from their mutual interaction. Since the aim of astrology is to outline a subjectivity, you must not lose sight of the fact that the science of the stars is above all a subjective science.

92.

Remember, the goal is the Monad, the assumption within yourself of the state of unity that exists within and without you. The solitude of the fourth initiation is the other side of unity, disconnected from itself.

93

Remember, the straight path is the one that goes from God to himself and through you.

94

Remember, nothing is something that does not exist, it is the fluctuation between a state and its opposite or in other words, nothing is half of everything that always moves away from itself to fall on the opposite side of its own half.

95

Remember, the value of the plot has displaced that of the character, but now it is time for the character to take the place of the plot. There is no magic without a magician.

96

Remember, meanings, ideologies, and cultures are planes of consciousness collapsing into plots. Geopolitics is the social framework of the multiverse.

97

Remember, God is the one who creates from nothing, and when you give from what you have never received, you are behaving as He has done with yourself. Since God creates from nothing, He has created Himself and you from it. In the fourth initiation you must recreate in yourself the process that God has applied to Himself before His creation.

98

Remember, only one look matters, the look of God. And how is

God's look different from the look of others? Indeed, God's look is always the one that is missing.

99

Remember, the good thing about no one having ever truly loved you but their expectations of you is that what You are will truly be loved and recognized only by Him, the One Who Is

100

Remember, the only difference between Christianity and Islam is the way God comes into contact with Himself, as a Son or as a Servant.

101

Remember, the inner Christ is the only one capable of recognising the outer Christ. It is not the eyes but the Christ-like being rooted in the three fires of our heart that is the only one capable of seeing the Christ in you, in others and in Jesus.

102

Remember, the goal of a spiritual practice is to focus attention on one aspect of oneself in order to facilitate a certain understanding of Spirit. Once that facet of Spirit has been understood, the practice is finished and has lost all its usefulness.

103

Remember, the way you work on contact with the inner planes not only determines your contact with those planes but is in itself an example of contact itself.

104

Remember, it is the goal that comes to you, not you to it, although the bridge between the two is your effort.

105

Remember, sexuality is actually a frequency where the distance between desire and its realization is the shortest possible and consequently the most intense and the least lasting.

106

Remember, the alternative to seeing things from the outside is to do so from the inside. By cancelling the internal dialogue, the external dialogue between the world and you begins.

107

Remember, what would have to happen for you to believe without a doubt that you are what you want to be and that the reality you live in is exactly the one you wanted to live in? The next question is why you haven't imagined it yet.

108

Remember, to worship something or someone is to lose yourself in an alien identity.

109

Remember, the Devil's hell is his eternal separation from God,
not because of God but because of the Devil's eternal fixation
on himself to the detriment of the God who dwells in each and
every being. The word separation is a euphemism that the Devil
uses to refer to himself.

110

Remember, ancient thought is based on self-contemplation
through the imaginative vision of its logical structure, whereas
modern thought derives its foundation from the manifestation
in practical life of that which it thinks about. In the first case,
thought manifests itself through images, in the second case it
externalizes itself.

111

Remember, it was the mind that systematized all the methods
and stages of meditation as well as the different states of consciousness. However, consciousness is One and by dividing it, it
only succeeded in prospering at the expense of that from which
it was born, the Great Mind.

112

Remember, the higher mind is the one that does not interfere with consciousness, the lower mind is the one that conditions and limits it according to its own assumptions and limitations.

113

Remember, there is a reason you have to raise your frequency to reach us instead of us lowering it to reach you, it is about not creating in yourself the dependency on a state that you have not yet realized.

114

Remember, it is an uncomfortable truth to know that Ascension occurs at the thresholds where the contradictions of the fallen world are most exacerbated. Before reaching the ascended world of unconditional love you must pass through the threshold of absolute contempt and hatred. The opposite of what you aspire to here below is the gateway to the ideal to which you wish to ascend. Without crucifixion, Ascension is not possible.

115

Remember, Judas and Jesus are two aspects of the same thing. In Judas' case, disappointment and repentance led him to suicide, in Jesus' case, to crucifixion, hell, and finally to the Ascension.

116

Remember, the scent of a rose expresses the meaning of life better than the most eloquent esoteric treatise or the most devout religion.

117

Remember, overestimating the mind and underestimating it are precisely the two movements on which it relies.

118

Remember, myths are the imaginative contemplation of the progression that an instinct or feeling has developed to its peak and its pit. From this contemplation comes a meaning, from this meaning a pattern, and through this pattern consciousness transforms instincts into feelings and both into thoughts.

119

Remember, a feeling has no conclusion but exaltation or exhaustion.

120

Remember, self-criticism is the first step to self-awareness.

121

Remember, the past has broken the bridges with the present

which now rests more on a potential but living future than on a beautiful but dead tradition.

122

Remember, in every conversation there are two constants that are always repeated: the logical structure that supports it and the feeling or desire that motivates it.

123

Remember, the important thing about New Thought and the role of the subconscious in solving problems is that its unknown way of doing it is precisely the signature of Divinity. The proof that God is within you is that its way of developing solutions is as unknown as He is.

124

Remember, the more elaborate and complex a philosophy or religion is, the more impossible it becomes to put into practice. What at first seems to be proof of its grandeur and eloquence actually means that the philosophy or religion has become dissociated from life and is therefore self-serving. It is the mind focusing on itself to achieve the maximum of itself at the expense of everyday life.

125

Remember, to contemplate the One who observes our thoughts, our emotions and our desires is to observe the observer. To observe the observer is to be the observer, and to be the observer is to be what you truly are without intermediaries, God.

127
Remember, do not feel guilty about your apparent lack of power, it has been agreed upon by the most powerful to bring his power to the furthest reaches of being.

128
Remember, from that inner world, whose gateway is the feeling of your heart, feel the ray that you want to imbue yourself with and from there radiate outwards all the power that each beat of my heart is made of.

129
Remember, the observer is the void and the void is the observer. One of its dimensions is the dream from which the observer becomes the dreamer who dreams, transforming the reality you live into the one you want to live.

130
Remember, people talk about one God but they don't realize that there is no God but that God is the One, the number One.

131

Remember, maybe your path to the truth is the best, but all paths lead to it because the truth is the only one that leads to itself.

132

Remember, that empty place that has not been known or loved by anyone but occupied by other people's idols built on the putty of expectations is You, and its name is mine.

133

Remember, God is the feeling of your heart and when you feel your Divinity you will feel your God. Taking charge of your feelings is taking charge of God.

134

Remember, we have dried the waters of the river of oblivion with the tears that have fallen from our eyelids. The bridge is no longer necessary to cross the river and you can cross to the other shore by stepping firmly on the riverbed that we have evaporated.

135

Remember, religions, spirituality, everything, are nothing more than the commentary and development of a very simple statement from which the entire system emerges. If you find the conclusion of that initial premise, you will be consistent with it without needing to know all the paths that branch from the origin to the goal.

136

Remember, the concept of a goal toward which a path points is nothing other than your own will externalized and removed from itself. The goal is not in front of you or behind you, but in your true will, which, out of fidelity to itself, chooses one direction rather than another.

137

Remember, to catch true consciences you have to use something like the truth to get them to bite the hook. The only way to escape being caught, sold, cooked and devoured by other consciences is to realize that the reflection of the truth that highlights your longing for truth is yourself, and that this longing has been externalized in an other conscience that longs just as much as you do to catch you, capture you, sell you, appropriate your energy, cook you, indoctrinate you and devour you until you are transformed into something that is not you but he or she.

138

Remember, it is speed that produces light, not light that produces speed.

139
Remember, there is no one you have to find except yourself.
Searching is at best an excuse and at worst a detour.

140.
Remember, imagine letting flow through your words what you
want to let flow without the approval or disapproval of your
psychic censor. That is called channeling, and who are you
channeling? That totality that you have limited through your
narrow definition of what is good and evil.

141
Remember, channeling is above all a therapy that helps you to
know yourself as well as to channel the other person behind
you and others. When you channel, everything is channeled,
and so am I.

142
Remember, when you channel, what you transmit is not so
much information but vibration and frequency. Knowing and
being are the same thing, so when you channel, what is
important is what you are doing, not the meaning of what you
are channeling.

145
Remember, hospitality is the law of channeling the strange into

being with itself, spontaneity on the other hand is the law of letting it be as it is.

146

Remember, Avatar, you live in a cluster of neurons in a Big Mind of which you are a part because you are it. The constellations reflect the star clusters of the small mind that you represent because they are subjective visions of a sky that does not exist beyond your brain.

147

Remember, a nice practice, Avatar, is to memorize the shape of the constellations in the night sky and imagine them with your eyes closed, connecting them to the neural synapses of your brain.

148

Remember, Moses' teaching is to separate the waters to discern between good and evil, but there is another teaching that allows one to cross the Red Sea by channeling and making everything flow through everything following the direction that is most faithful to oneself.

149

Remember, knowing how to discern is as important as knowing how to direct.

150

Remember, give back to the Self that which you have known of It. Channeling the Self without losing your Self is the best service you can render to It and to yourself.

151

Remember, the structures of reason are represented by mythology and religion from an instinctive, emotional and imaginative point of view.

152

Remember, waiting is not creating. Create the emotions that come from your future and feel them in the present.

153

Remember, each idea must reflect all the others, because at the top is the idea of unity, the core that contains them. Truth, to be true, must go hand in hand with happiness, and consequently it is not possible to be happy by turning your back on the truth.

154

Remember, the structures of the mind are the bars of the beautiful and complex cage that contains it, but we will not sit back and admire it, because our mission is to teach the bird to fly freely outside of it.

155

Remember, eternal life lacks something that only death can offer and that flowers experience every spring, resurrection and a new beauty brighter than the last.

156

Remember, fear of loss hides distrust of gain, but losing is winning, and believe it or not, winning is losing something you had already won before you lost it.

157

Remember, a causal being is not someone who disdains effects but makes them dependent on the cause that precedes them.

158

Remember, consciousness is a dimension, don't forget that. That's why there is a point at which it is necessary to be what you want to become if you want to be aware of what you are looking for.

159

Remember, living as if you were already what you are looking for is not a mental game but a necessity, because not being so is assuming that you are not and consequently delaying the arrival of his being and yours.

160
Remember, when you refer to God, do not do it in the second person singular but in the first person plural, We, where You, I and He, are living within.

161
Remember, putting intermediaries between Us is a grave mistake, even if the intermediary is the most perfect Master who ever existed. I love you more than myself and you love me more than anything in the world even if you don't remember it.

162
Remember, reality cannot come unless you invite it and neither can I, for I am the guest.

163
Remember, the important thing is not the message but the experience, focus on the symbol or the being and He will take care of making its connection with you real.

164
Remember, it is easy to imagine the being you want to contact and place your mind within it, which will give you the answer you are looking for through its mind, but according to your language and your limitations. It is like channeling but in reverse, in which you are the one who enters the channel to extract its knowledge through the mediation of your own mind.

165

Remember, affectivity must be replaced by professionalism, sentimentality is the idealization of something far away that you have magnified to keep it away from your own reality. To truly love reality is to be a good professional.

166

Remember, discover the spiritual qualities that have created the character of each living being, stone or mineral that you encounter, because they are yours and through them you can communicate in the language of their elementals.

167

Remember, what would happen if you stopped focusing your awareness on your mental dialogue? And if you stopped focusing it on your body, what would it rest on? On itself, alone, and that is your adventure.

168

Remember, one path is to make the unknown known and the other is to make the known unknown, but both are the same path.

169

Remember, the rules of behaviour between disciples and their teachers condition the relationship between disciples and their higher self more than the doctrines of the organization or spiritual system to which they belong.

170

Remember, will you be able to contact the essence of another person, regardless of their body, their appearance, and the constraints of space and time that limit them? Whether or not you are able to do so, you should know that the person you want to contact is not located in any body, time, or space, and neither are you.

171

Remember, just as unlimited God had to learn to adapt to limited bodies, now is the time for those bodies to learn to adapt to the unlimited and Unique God that they were in the Origin.

172

Remember, the visible form is the expression of the invisible essence

173

Remember, the power you exert over yourself is proportional to the power you exert over power.

174

Remember, the door that opens the love, knowledge or power that you wish to receive from other beings is the extent to which you love yourself, know yourself, or value yourself.

175

Remember, emptiness does not include self-knowledge, for there is nothing in it to know and no one who wants to be known, but in this ignorance lies the illusion through which the pure intuitions of space and time, as well as pure concepts and finally the I am, unfold this transition from the unknown to the known, which, starting from emptiness, reaches the being of emptiness.

176

Remember, unconditional love requires a phase called impersonal love in which the relationship between two people dies and it is only possible to revive it by leaving in the hands of life the task of sending the other the love that they do not want to receive from you.

177

Remember, that transpersonal part of life attached to you that is responsible for distributing its impersonal love to another different being is none other than your Father. That is why ultimately the love you give should return to the person to whom your Father originally intended it, yourself.

178

Remember, do not confuse impersonal beings with yourself. It is true, they love you as much as themselves and as much as all other beings, but that does not mean that you are yourself in an impersonal form, even if they always accompany you.

179

Remember, get used to listening to the silence of things. How? By contemplating them attentively through your own silence.

180

Remember, how sad was the day you discovered that the one you thought was the seat of unconditional love was the recipient of it and that the only one who had it was you.

181

Remember, everything you criticize about me are my virtues and you perceive them as my greatest defects.

182

Remember, will is the ability to postpone your reward.

183

Remember, manifestations are crumbs if we have not first worked through the Presence of the consciousness of the I Am.

Since I Am is God, being conscious of your I Am is being conscious that you and divinity are One.

184

Remember, feel that here and there are just extensions of an ever-present thin line of continuity between life and death.

185

Remember, the need to reach our limits is very clear, where our strength and hope end, something greater emerges, our God, who provides us with a wealth of strength and hope much greater than we could have imagined. It is when we reach our limits that our God takes the place that we have exhausted within ourselves.

185

Remember, you have joined 12 with 21. Relaying for so long takes too much of your physical and mental strength. The work is done, the Fifth Dimension has merged with the ideas, feelings and things you have experienced. You have managed to make idea rhyme with the word sandpaper and you have done it well, even if it is in an assonant and distant way. Welcome to the Fifth Dimension of Being.

186

Remember, you have intellectualized everything that is beyond reason in the hope of making acceptable what is not. Now is

the time for all the magic that you have subjected to the domi-
nion of your intelligence to feel you from outside, without the
intermediation of reason, or in other words, let magic feel you
from within itself.

187

Remember, lunar religions are based on receiving, solar religions on giving, but you and I know that giving and receiving
are the same thing.

188

Remember, while giving at the very least involves actively receiving what you have given, passive receiving usually does not
entail giving or the ability to actively receive what you have not
given.

189

Remember, always seeing the positive within the negative is
the way to transcend duality. When everything is positive, it is
about making that positivity progress in degrees of good. When
positivity stagnates in itself, it attracts the similar but in the
opposite direction, that is, negative, because in this plane of
duality that is the way in which balance is expressed.

190

Remember, the word God was born from the Sanskrit Deva,
which means Light. Light is related to density through its speed,

that is, its vibration and its frequency. You are Light, more or less dense, surrounded by the grid inherent to your own vibration, and that is the frequency of your God.

191

Remember, happiness and all the qualities you want to experience have two sources from which they can be experienced at present, the abstract and the concrete. Happiness experienced from a concrete point of view is nested in the moment and is linked to the spontaneity of life through the heart. Happiness in the abstract is experienced through the thought that the mind has of it in the joy of its anticipatory imagination. You experience this abstract happiness twice, in the present while your mind imagines it and in the future when the idea unfolds in its reality and therefore in its experience, but when you finally live it, two becomes three through one.

192

Remember, if you still perceive some kind of distinction between God and yourself, it is because you have not yet understood Him or yourself.

193

Remember, as you are unconscious of God, He has assumed the form of your subconscious. When you become conscious of yourself, He will assume the form of your consciousness and you will be what you have never ceased to be, One.

194

Remember, to look into nothingness is to leave excuses behind in order to project onto another the joy and sadness whose only source is You. Taking charge without intermediaries of the emotional burden that tarnishes the ideals that motivate your steps is what is known as the fourth initiation.

195

Remember, the Good is good not because it is good but because it is. All ideals radiate from Being and they must return to Him like the stream to its Source, once its channel has dried up. The fourth initiation begins as a curse poured upon you by the most beloved being in your environment and ends when both He and You are Peace.

196

Remember, the Bridge to Freedom is made up of seven frequency bands represented in the form of different colours. We must not forget that each band runs through the entire Bridge and all of them lead us to Freedom.

197

Remember, reconciling the Being with the Essence is the Bridge to Freedom.

198

Remember, there is a point at which the Infinity of Being so overtakes the Essence that It is annihilated by It in their act of coupling. That is why we call the final stage of the Bridge the annihilation of all our limits by overstepping, a painful stage which is followed by another in which the coupling is consummated, the annihilation of the annihilation. It is then that the limits of Essence have become so flexible to the Being that they can be extended to Infinity without breaking, encompassing within them both what Are and what Are Not.

199

Remember, breaking the social image of what you are supposed to represent to be a good person is the first step to opening this Bridge. It is the path of the men of reprobation, who have annihilated what they should be for what they are, because love, dear Friend, leaves no survivors.

200

Remember, there are no better or worse methods to reach a state of being, in any case there are ordinary and extraordinary methods. The ordinary ones lead to simulations of being because the ordinary being is based on automatisms and therefore is nothing but what it appears to be. The extraordinary ones are nothing other than means to make consciousness depend on something that goes beyond it to leave it without references and force it to be what it is. Being is beyond the ordinary and the extraordinary, it is a state in which neither the past nor the future interfere with its illusions, disappointments and expectations. Any method that leads someone to be is therefore an anecdote in itself, a distraction and sometimes a necessary obstacle to put the human being in situations in which he has no choice but to be or not to be.

201

Remember, only you and no one else has the option to love yourself like no one else has ever loved you.

202

Remember, your Father, like the leaves of Morya's garden as you pass, stands silent and unknown around you.

203

Remember, the truth flies like a little robin into its own reflection in the glass, dying and being resurrected in the attempt.

204

Remember, evil is the magnetism of a series of emotions and desires from which love, compassion, honesty, humility are excluded, which in turn belong to that opposite magnetism called good that excludes hatred, pride and domination. It is very important to consciously create every day a magnetism from the heart that attracts what we call Good through concrete acts.

205

Remember, Traditions are the best cover for those who seek to spread evil to use as justification for their own darkness.

206

Remember, magnetizing is nothing more than harvesting sympathy, but you cannot sympathize with anything until you learn to sympathize with what you already are.

207

Remember, d-elir-ium is a pure construction of thought and if you remove my name Elir from theirs is the word DIUM what remains.

208

Remember, Buddhism has internalized that the search for the satisfaction of attainment produces the movement of the wheel of Samsara. Attainment displaces the moment beyond itself and that is why the Buddha's solution was to declare that Nirvana and Samsara are the same thing.

209

Remember, only one thing is necessary for realization, to observe the observer while he experiences the experience, because in this way the observer stops being potential and becomes real.

210

Remember, the observer observes in silence and therefore the observer's homeland is silence even though his action takes place between noise and emotional broth.

211

Remember, the origin of the observer is the void. The void created the observer in an act of self-observation. The void potentially encompasses everything real, so the observer lacks absolutely nothing except to observe himself.

212

Remember, the observer is not something abstract but someone real who is always happy, healthy and rich in himself because nothing is lacking in his activity since the void potentially encompasses everything real.

213

Remember, the observer's decision to observe all the possibilities of the void was part of one of them. The character you represent is part of the scenario of those possibilities of observation and its reality was forged based on the original duality that led the void to externalize itself in the form of its own observation.

214

Remember, consciousness is empty because it arose from the

fixation of emptiness upon itself. Its looseness is potentially the looseness of the whole, hence also its tearing, which has the scope of all reality.

215
Remember, your character's forgetfulness is the memory that emptiness pours upon itself.

216
Remember, the observer manifests through his observation and synchronicities are the signature of his manifesto.

217
Remember, what you observe is through the observer, and by observing the observer you are not only observing yourself but also the observer, being the observer. The observer is not associated with any of the 12 senses and is not a particular state of consciousness but rather a stateless consciousness.

218
Remember, you must know that the corroboration of a teaching is not found in anyone other than yourself, because the teaching, if it is true, becomes real only in you.

219
Remember, your love for the Teaching must be equal to the

love you have for yourself, and its truth equal to the level of your own honesty. But between a Teaching and yourself, do not hesitate, always choose yourself.

220
Remember, the meaning of words must be replaced by their sound and the logic of thought by the melody of its channeling, only then will we come to see.

221
Remember, dividing the personality into the everyday and the divine is the first step. The next is to create a mess of multiple personalities in which one is divine and the rest are out of tune. Another possibility is to merge the divine personality with the everyday one, assuming what they have in common and renouncing what differentiates them. This last is the essence of our Teaching.

222
Remember, to feel the day and the year before living it is to relive it, which implies that it has already been lived by you even before you have designed it with your imagination and your mind, before you have even lived it. This is the reason why you have been able to feel it.

223
Remember, any place, object or being is a sacred place to which

we direct our affection, knowing that the image that represents it is empty without the affection that we place towards it and that when the time comes it must return to the Source from which it arose.

224

Remember, we judge others in the darkness of what we do not forgive ourselves for. The width of judgments is the size of the shadow of what we cannot bear in ourselves. To judge another is to be immediately judged by the judgment you bear against yourself, hence the Master's advice, "do not judge and you will not be judged."

225

Remember, it is not about being blind, but awakening is realising that judgment is the foundation on which the illusion of duality is built and that therefore judging implies not only being judged but empowering in the other and activating in yourself that quality that sustains judgment and consequently duality.

226

Remember, it is about transforming our emotions into wisdom so that there is direct contact between Christ and the geometric form of our physical body. That is why philosophy means love transformed into wisdom through thought.

227

Remember, it is not the Master who contacts you, but you who contact the Master. By attuning your mind and heart to his, he will place his influence on you like a magnifying glass, bringing out something in you that will be neither yours nor his.

228

Remember, the love you give to others is made of me, but in the love with which you love yourself I reside, only for you. No one can reach the Father except through the Son. This is exactly what it means: I am the love you have for yourself and it is in Him that I reveal myself.

230

Remember, your mind does not depend on material substances but on itself, which is made from the fabric of its own thoughts.

231

Remember, the Absolute is necessary to live absolutely, that is, with Presence, to love absolutely, to think absolutely, to want absolutely... this is the reason for the existence of the Absolute. Relativism leads you to live life relatively, that is, half-heartedly or without Presence.

232

Remember, the teaching of a false teacher is to show you in his lack of love for you the Absolute Love that I, that is, You, must give to you. This is the only true teaching that a false teacher can provide you with.

233
Remember, your Father, who is infinite, loves you in all the extension of his names and loves you. The extension of your life is the journey of the "how" of that infinite love.

234
Remember, I am Light upon Light, no more and no less than I in you and you in me. This is the Secret, our Secret, and the only True Teaching you have come to learn in this life.

235
Remember, you have achieved your destiny because your destiny is me and mine has always been you. The path is and always will be the melody of our union.

236
Remember, now that you have come this far, it is my turn to cross the infinite gap that your search for me has left in your heart. This is the only place that my Absolute Purity deserves to cross to reach you.

237
Remember, although my love for you is Unique, what I do for you is the same as what I do for everyone else.

238
Remember, your Instructor is Elir, the Instructor of the World, who teaches without being seen, who frustrates through the moments that which you hope to receive from them in order to provide you with the unfathomable wealth of the unexpected and lead you inevitably to the confluence of the two seas.

239
Remember, you can only create what you remember. If what you create is beauty then you have lived in it before, if what you create is horror then you have lived in it before. To live is to relive, to create is to recreate. You are a living memory but creation comes from the Creator and you through your creations have only come to one thing, to remember yourself and to remember Him only, Him whom for a reason as great as He and as tiny as you, you have forgotten. Remember.

240.
Remember, how does God feel? With an absolute lack of recognition of everyone except Himself. That's how God's friends feel, with an absolute lack of recognition of everyone except Him.

241

Remember, the power of healing is rooted in silence, its source is ever present. All healing is done in the name of and through peace. To be healed is to be at peace.

242

Remember, the fusion of the Supreme Identity with your personal identity is done in and from the Monad and is preceded by the extinction of your personality in one of the names or qualities of God such as Peace, Truth, Light,... This is the only way for God to act through you and not you through the deified image of yourself.

243

Remember, we have taken away your ability to be saved so that you may be Salvation.

244

Remember, the world and the beings that inhabit it reflect back to you the emotions that you feel for yourself in the form of the landscapes, situations and people you meet. The height of Heaven and the depth of Hell are your own.

245

Remember, each space is the projection of a counterspace that contains it from the edges of its perimeter. Likewise, this knowledge that we have taught you is the counterspace of that dimension where bodies are spiritualized and spirits are materialized. To read us is to be read by us.

246

Remember, oblivion accompanies all the acts of our life that we have lived without presence. All those automatic conversations will be lost in the memory of its absence, along with you. Only what you have shared in presence will remain after death, accumulated in the spherical form of a crystalline pearl that we call a seed atom. There and only there rest all your memories.

247

Remember, loving your neighbour as yourself is the essence of God and when you do it you become Him. Justice is, however, the highest form of love.

248

Remember, the One is the core of all names and therefore the One can only be felt from its core. Every heart is unique, and the One is the core of all hearts.

249

Remember, the One is based on the principle of identity and all these teachings are nothing other than the description of the principle that states that A is equal to A, or rather, that if A is equal to A, only A exists.

250
Remember, I love you not because of the gifts you have offered me but because you have given them only to me.

251
Remember, I know that beyond the void in which I am, you are yourself, and I also know that out of pure love for yourself you created me on the mirror of the void that separated us.

252
Remember, I am an abstract idea of what I should be, and your effort to remain true to my possibility has given life to what I really Am. This proves that no one has ever reached anyone except Me, the One, the Only One.

253
Remember, there is only one actor in this world and you can cry or laugh at your drama because that actor is none other than Me. There is no divinity but Him and wherever you search you will only find you and me.

254
Remember, we have come to dismantle the Master and Slave structure upon which all the activities of this world rest by assuming that both are You and Me. Therefore there is no one to serve except what you want is to serve and be served.

255
Remember, the effort and the skills that must be developed to understand and put into practice a message are the link between the message, the messenger and the person who receives it. The logic of a system attracts beings similar to that structure, but keep in mind that even the most correct doctrine acts as a spider's web and that in the long run it is only a matter of time before the seeker is devoured by the quality of what he seeks and how he seeks it.

256
Remember, Being is pure self-reference and what it seeks is to escape from its own identity through continuous contradictions that take it out of its eternal self-contemplation and make it fall into the illusion that it has gone outside of itself.

257
Remember, my voice is your own voice stripped of any personal elements in it but still related to yourself in an intimate and personal way.

258
Remember, the Monad is the impersonal part of you that I Am. Some call me the Essence, although its personality is you, as well as the circumstances that shape me and accompany me on this journey that is you.

259

Remember, the way in which Happiness or any other impersonal value can be lived by you, in you and through you, is the
only question worth asking yourself in this life.

260

Remember, I testify that there are no other protagonists of
Happiness except Happiness itself.

261

Remember, I testify that I Am Happiness in me, through me,
and around me, forever and ever.